3.

IRELAND

IRELAND

Ray Bonds

CHARTWELL
BOOKS, INC.

Published in 2009 by Compendium Publishing,
43 Frith Street, London W1D 4SA, United Kingdom.

CHARTWELL BOOKS, INC.
A Division of
BOOK SALES, INC.
276 Fifth Avenue Suite 206
New York, New York 10001

ISBN 13: 978-0-7858-2533-3
ISBN 10: 0-7858-2533-9

Design: Ian Welch/Peran Publishing Services

All Internet site information provided was correct when provided by the Author. The
Publisher can accept no responsibility for this information becoming incorrect.

Printed in China through Printworks Int . Ltd.

PAGE 1: Doo Lough in County Mayo.
(The Irish Image Collection/Corbis/42-19013079)

PAGES 2: Dunguaire Castle, Galway Bay.
(Tito Slack/iStockphoto/1073546)

PAGES 4-5: St. Kevin's monastery, County Wicklow.
(Bertrand Rieger/Hemis/Corbis/42-19834693)

OVER PAGE: The observation point above the Giant's
Causeway.
(Atlantide Phototravel/Corbis/42-18208671)

Contents

Introduction

Introduction

Ireland is also called the "Emerald Isle" for its lush vegetation and green countryside, the result of its mild, changeable, Oceanic climate, with frequent rainfalls and few extremes. The hottest it's ever been is 91.94°F, and the coldest -2.38°F, both recorded in the 1880s, when the driest-ever year (with only fourteen inches of rain) was also recorded.

The island is a little over 32,590 square miles in area, and is essentially a ring of coastal mountains surrounding low central plains. The highest mountain, at about 3,415 feet, is Carrauntoohil, County Kerry, in the southwest. Here and in the western counties the terrain is mountainous and rocky, with the least arable land in Ireland, although, almost by way of compensation, the panoramic vistas are spectacular and are a great attraction to tourists. The west is somewhat wetter than other parts of the island, and also experiences violent and destructive Atlantic storms that are liable to bring high winds, heavy rainfall, snow, and hail.

Ireland is surrounded by the Atlantic Ocean to the west and the Irish Sea to the east. Of its nine-hundred-mile coastline, it is the western part that is the most spectacular. Stretching from north Clare to south Galway, The Burren includes miles of limestone layers cut through by meandering streams, lakes, and labyrinthine caves.

More than seventy percent of Ireland's native flora is to be found here, and the region is also home to more than 500 ringforts and 80 Neolithic tombs. The coast here features towering cliffs, clear fresh waters, and pristine sandy beaches, and is a vast playground for water sports enthusiasts, while at the same time being home to a wide range of fishing villages offering some of the best seafood in the world.

The River Shannon, longest of all in Ireland (and Great Britain), runs more or less north to south, starting at the Shannon Pot on the slopes of the Cuilcagh mountains in County Cavan to Loop Head in County Clare, where it meets the Atlantic. Rich in glorious scenery, filled with prolific wildlife, and dotted with pretty villages, the Shannon Erne Waterway is the longest navigable waterway in Europe, and is a paradise for nature lovers, boating enthusiasts, and those who prefer the quiet life.

Off the coast there are scores of islands and rocky outcrops. On some of them, islanders eke out just enough of a living for subsistence, enjoying simple but often very hard lives—many of the islands didn't have electricity until the 1970s. At the other end of the financial scale, exploration is underway to exploit an important natural gas deposit off the northwest coast; estimates suggest the yield could be as much as 30 billion cubic meters, some seventy percent of the volume of the Kinsale Head gas field of the 1990s.

There are two ecoregions in Ireland, the Celtic broadleaf forests and North Atlantic moist mixed forests. Ireland supports fewer wildlife and plant species than are found in Britain and mainland Europe, the reason being, apparently, that it became an island shortly after the end of the last glacial period some 10,000 years ago. There are only about twenty-five land mammal species native to Ireland because it was rapidly isolated from Europe by rising sea levels after the Ice Age.

The long history of agricultural production, especially coupled with modern intensive farming methods, has had an impact on wildlife. "Runoff" of contaminants into streams, rivers, and lakes affect the natural freshwater ecosystems. A land of green fields for crop cultivation and cattle rearing limits the space available for the establishment of native wild species. Hedgerows, however, traditionally used for maintaining and demarcating land boundaries, act as a refuge for native wild flora. Their ecosystems stretch across the countryside and act as a network of connections to preserve remnants of the ecosystem that once covered the island.

Humans first settled in Ireland from about 8000 B.C., and by 200 B.C. the island had become dominated by Celtic migration and influence. During those thousands of years tribes from Southern Europe had established a high Neolithic culture, the best-known Neolithic sites in Ireland being the megalithic passage-tombs of Newgrange and Knowth in County Meath (both c.3200 B.C.).

The Middle Ages witnessed relatively small-scale settlement, first by the Vikings and then the Normans, but this gave way to complete English domination by the 1600s. Protestant English rule led to marginalization of the Catholic majority.

The Wars of the Three Kingdoms (of which the English Civil War became the best known) were a series of conflicts involving the Irish, Scottish, and English between 1639 and 1651 over religious and civil issues. Ultimately, the English Parliament (led by Oliver Cromwell) won the day over the English monarch, the Irish, and the Scots. Cromwell's conquest of Ireland became known as the Irish Confederate Wars, and helped to determine the future of Great Britain as a constitutional monarchy with political power centered on London. Cromwell's actions against the Irish were brutal in the extreme, and many historians have claimed that the Parliamentary campaign resulted in the death or exile of between fifteen and twenty percent of the Irish population (some reports suggest that 600,000 people, almost half the population, died).

Tragedy revisited Ireland in the mid-1700s and again in the mid-1800s, in what came to be called the "Great Famines." First, it is believed that in 1740 and 1741 extreme cold and wet

weather in successive years ruined the harvest, and the combination of starvation and a range of diseases led to ten percent of Ireland's population dying.

Second was the famine of 1845–1852, the repercussions of which were far greater and longer lasting than that of a hundred years earlier. This time, as a result of a potato blight, more than a million people died from starvation and diseases, and over two million emigrated—in all, between twenty and twenty-five percent of Ireland's population.

Tragic enough though such drastic emigration was, more problems lay in wait down the years, even up to today: under the Constitution of Ireland, loosely interpreted, and with many caveats, certain descendants of those who emigrated may qualify for the right to register as Irish citizens, and to live there. Today, this could involve up to 80 million people from around the world! Understandably, what has been called the "Irish Diaspora" has led to much political consternation and discussion.

Following the defeat by Cromwell's forces in the Irish Rebellion of 1641, and further discord over the next sixty years, various laws were passed that disadvantaged the Irish Catholic community in Ireland. Despite the fact that ninety percent of Ireland's population was native Irish Catholic, none of these people could sit in the Parliament of Ireland. However, toward the end of the eighteenth century the Irish Parliament (which was entirely Protestant) gained a greater degree of independence from the British Parliament than ever before. Certain Protestants (called "dissenters") joined Catholics in a rebellion led by the Society of United Irishmen, with the aim of creating a fully independent republican state. But the rebellion was put down by British forces in 1798. In 1801 the Kingdom of Ireland and the Kingdom of Great Britain were merged to form the United Kingdom of Great Britain and Ireland, ruled directly by the U.K. Parliament in London.

Meanwhile, mass emigration continued, and the population has never returned to the pre-famine level of over eight million (as recorded in the 1841 census).

During the nineteenth and early twentieth centuries support for Irish nationalism among the Roman Catholic population was gaining ground, and armed rebellion ensued, notably the Easter Rising of 1916 and the Irish War of Independence of 1919. In 1921 the Anglo-Irish Treaty was entered into by the British government and the leaders of the Irish Republic, recognizing a two-state solution. Fearing dominance by Catholic and Southern Irish interests, Northern Ireland, with a majority Protestant population (but including a significant Catholic and nationalist minority), opted for remaining part of the United Kingdom instead of forming a home rule state. Disagreement concerning provisions of the treaty led to the Irish Civil War, which ended in defeat for anti-treaty forces in 1923.

The Irish Free State, formed in 1922 under the Anglo-Irish Treaty, comprised the whole of Ireland until the Northern Ireland opt-out. It replaced Southern Ireland and the self-proclaimed Irish Republic, and its new government also replaced both the Provisional Government of Southern Ireland and the Government of the Irish Republic. In 1937 the Irish Free State was renamed Éire.

"The Troubles" was a period of ethno-political conflict in Northern Ireland from the late 1960s to the late 1990s. The main issues were the constitutional status of Northern Ireland and the relationship between the mainly-Protestant Unionist and mainly-Catholic Nationalist communities in Northern Ireland. There were many riots and much violence, including devastating bomb attacks, internments and hunger strikes, then paramilitary ceasefires, and a military stalemate.

Eventually, the Belfast Agreement (also called the Good Friday Agreement) came into effect on December 2, 1999. Among its many provisions were that any change to the constitutional status of Northern Ireland could only follow a majority vote of its citizens, and that all parties would commit to exclusively peaceful and democratic means to resolve issues.

Today, there are two political entities in the island of Ireland: the sovereign country of Ireland (also known as the Republic of Ireland) covering five-sixths of the island, with its capital in Dublin; and Northern Ireland, part of the United Kingdom of Great Britain and Northern Ireland covering the sixth, with its capital in Belfast. There are four provinces: Connacht, Leinster, Munster, and Ulster. There are twenty-six counties in the Republic, and six in Northern Ireland.

In a number of instances there are "all-island" institutions that transcend constitutional divisions. Generally, but not exclusively, the island operates as a single unit in major religious denominations and an increasing number of economic fields. There are also all-island circumstances that relate to some sports such as hurling, Gaelic football, rugby and others, but not soccer, where the Irish Football Association retains control only in Northern Ireland and a separate Football Association of Ireland controls the remainder.

In spite of all the political disruption, the conflict, and historic "troubles" outlined above, Ireland is a beautiful country in which to live and to visit. Ireland's population is about 6.1 million people, with 4.35 million in the Republic and 1.75 million in Northern Ireland. As has been noted, Ireland has experienced high levels of emigration. However, the country's high standard of living and membership of the European Union (EU) since 1973 have attracted quite significant numbers of immigrants from other EU member states and other countries looking for work. Notable among them have been more than 150,000 Polish people since 2004, and over 100,000 Chinese.

By far the biggest influx of people to the island, though, has been tourists from overseas.

During the year 2007 they swelled the population by more than nine million and contributed mightily to the already healthy economy. And no wonder—for there's so much to see and do in Ireland, north to south, east to west.

Most people will arrive in Ireland by air, flying into one of the five main international airports. There are several smaller regional airports that generally offer services between Irish destinations or between these and the U.K. Another favored means of getting to and from the island is to drive onto one of the ferry services operating between Ireland and the U.K. or mainland Europe.

Once in Ireland visitors will find an extensive network of rail services, including a new and expanding light rail system called Luas, and an extensive, developing road system giving access to all of the fabulous areas of interest.

Ireland is an island of great contrasts, particularly with regard to its scenery. On the coast, sheer craggy cliffs drop down onto wide sandy beaches. Hill walkers will scale a mountain from which the grand vista may be a gloriously peaceful lake, or a river bubbling through a town into a quaint fishing harbor. Drivers may have to give way to sheep being herded through a colorfully painted village; or around the next bend they may encounter a festival or a dance competition in progress, or a march celebrating an historic event (the Irish do so love their marches!).

If fishing is their scene they could be rewarded with a surprise catch of salmon or trout. Or they may enjoy a round of golf surrounded by nature's finest scenery on one of the incredible links courses that have been designed to test even championship professionals.

Tourists can hunt down graceful stately homes and gardens to visit, or photograph tiny thatched farm cottages to show the folks back home. Visitors won't be able to resist the warm welcome they will receive in a country or city pub, where musicians perform the songs of their forebears while diners enjoy some of the best food and drink in the world. If they choose the right time of year to travel they can take in an opera or their favorite ballet, or cram into the Slane for a top international rock music performance.

As they say, "Enjoy the craic!"

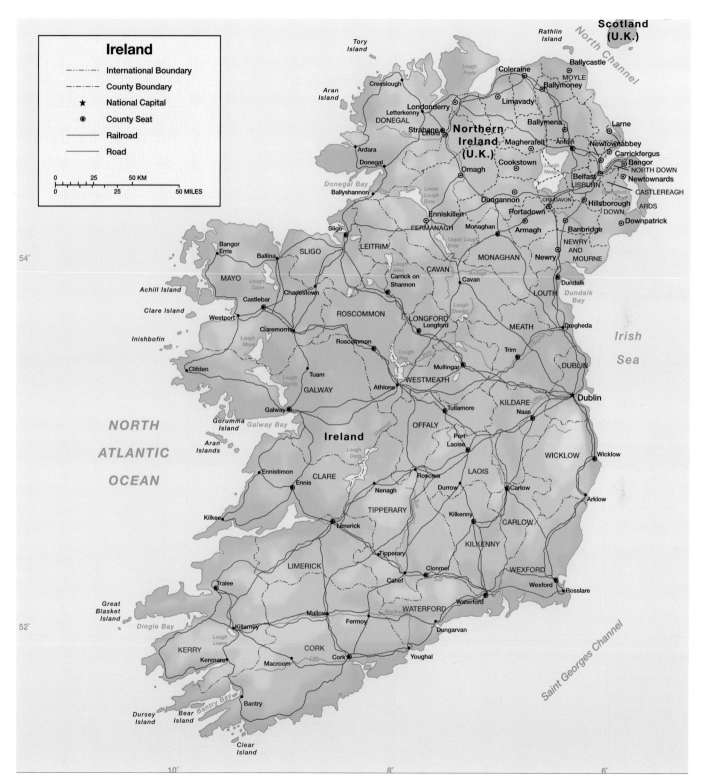

FAR LEFT: The Cliffs of Moher, at the southwestern edge of The Burren in County Clare, rise to about 700 feet above the Atlantic Ocean. (Ron Sumners/iStockphoto/3652954)

LEFT: Some farmers in Ireland eke out a hard living using agricultural practices that are generations-old. Here, stacks of turf are drying in the sun in a peat bog in County Mayo. (Jane McIlroy/iStockphoto/4400228)

RIGHT: The Giant's Causeway in County Antrim is made up of about 40,000 basalt columns, formed over a long period of igneous activity more than sixty million years ago. (Marco Testa/iStockphoto/6957362)

FAR LEFT: The Northern Ireland Parliament Buildings at Stormont, Belfast, now the home of the Northern Ireland Assembly that was created under the Belfast Agreement (also known as the Good Friday Agreement). This was signed in 1998, leading to direct London rule coming to an end, and political power being devolved to the new Assembly. (Robert Mayne/iStockphoto/5100984)

LEFT: A warm welcome awaits you in O'Donoghue's Bar, Dublin, where, frequently refreshed by pints of Guinness, local bands perform traditional music. (Patrick Nairne/fotoLibra/440029)

INTRODUCTION

LEFT: The Luas light rail or tram system serves Dublin. It has two lines (with two more under construction) and thirty-six stations, and operates on fifteen miles of track.
(Paul McNamara/fotoLibra/46053)

OVER PAGE: Tranquil waters close to Kerrykeel, a small village in County Donegal, between Knockalla Mountain and the picturesque Mulroy Bay, and precious little else other than fabulous views looking out to the Atlantic Ocean.
(Andrew Horsman/fotoLibra/4955588)

19

Coast and Islands

Coast and Islands

Ireland has over nine hundred miles of spectacular coastline, ranging from towering, craggy cliffs to wide sandy beaches. The western coastline in particular is rugged, with many islands, peninsulas, headlands, and bays. To the west is the gray, frequently wild Atlantic Ocean—next stop, the Americas. To the east, separating Ireland from Great Britain, is the Irish Sea, which is connected to the Atlantic by the Celtic Sea in the south via St. George's Channel between Ireland and Wales, and to the north by the North Channel between Northern Ireland and Scotland. There is no tunnel or bridge connecting Ireland to Great Britain and thence mainland Europe, although for years there has been much discussion about boring a fifty-mile rail tunnel to link Ireland and Britain, and a twenty-one-mile bridge/tunnel has frequently been seriously mooted.

Around the coast of Ireland there are more than seventy-five smaller islands ranging from rocky outcrops to inhabited and industrialized islands. The largest is Achill Island, about twelve miles long and wide, off the coast of County Mayo in the northwest. It has some 3,000 residents and is connected to the "mainland" by a 740-foot-long bridge. The Aran Islands (Inishmore, Inishmann, and Inisheer) in Galway Bay are probably the best known, with Inishmore (the largest) having a well-developed tourist industry. As with most of the other inhabited islands, attractions include many watersports, hill walking, rock climbing, angling, bird watching, and golf. (In addition, there are very many small islands on lakes/loughs and rivers, but see separate section.)

FAR RIGHT: Loop Head, on the north side of the River Shannon's estuary, juts out into the Atlantic. There is a lighthouse as well as a Loran aerial to warn shipping of the dangers posed by the cliffs and rocks.
(Stephen Power/fotoLibra/495467)

RIGHT: A few miles northward along the Loop Head cliffs, at the popular resort of Kilkee, youngsters enjoy the last of the fabulous sunset in one of the safest bathing spots in Europe.
(John Lennon/fotoLibra/160384)

FAR LEFT: The Cliffs of Moher, County Clare, rise to over 700 feet above the Atlantic. In 1835 Sir Cornelius O'Brien, a descendant of Ireland's High King Brian Boru, built a round, stone observation tower (which bears his name) from which tourists could enjoy the spectacular views. (Vernon Parker/fotoLibra/444248)

LEFT: Rolling waves crash against rocks at Connemara, County Galway, where there are a number of peninsulas protruding out into the Atlantic, as well as many small, rocky islands. (Saturar/iStockphoto/5582498)

RIGHT: The larger of the Skellig islands, Great Skellig (the other being Little Skellig) once housed a sixth century Christian monastery. Located off Bolus Head, County Kerry, the islands now play host to thousands of seabirds, in particular gannets and puffins.
(Michael St. Maur Sheil/Corbis/SH002362)

FAR RIGHT: The two Skelligs are about a mile apart, and about ten miles from the mainland. The Skellig lighthouse on Skellig Michael (an alternative name for Great Skellig) reminds shipping of the dangers of coming too close to the coast of southwest Ireland.
(Richard Cummins/Corbis/CU001404)

FAR LEFT: The quaint little fishing village of Kinvara, County Galway, now home to fewer than a thousand people as a result of the "Great Famine" of the 1840s and periodic emigrations up to the 1960s. (Tito Slack/iStockphoto/1107800)

LEFT: A few cottages here and there make up the former copper-mining village of Allihies in Ballydonegan Bay, County Cork, which suffered much emigration following the collapse in the price of copper in the mid-1800s. (S. Greg Panosian/iStockphoto/4329663)

LEFT: Mount Mweelrea, some 2,650 feet above sea level, is considered a fairly easy climb for novices, who are rewarded with fabulous views over Counties Mayo and Galway, as well as the Atlantic Ocean. (Frazer Ashford/fotoLibra/495670)

RIGHT: Fishing boats moored in Castletownbere (also known as Castletown Berehaven) in the southwest of County Cork, about to be lashed by rain-filled clouds.
(Philippa Wood/fotoLibra/493515)

FAR RIGHT: Fishing boats languish in the port of Greencastle, County Donegal, during a decline in the commercial fishing industry. One of Greencastle's main customers, throughout the Cold War of the 1950s to the 1990s, was the Soviet Union.
(Leslie Denman/fotoLibra/171131)

LEFT: In days gone by Kildavnet Tower guarded the approach to County Mayo's Achill Island, the largest of all Ireland's islands, which is joined to the mainland by the Michael Davitt Bridge, named after the nineteenth century political activist. (Frazer Ashford/fotoLibra/492738)

RIGHT: Scientists say that the basaltic columns that form the Giant's Causeway in County Antrim resulted from volcanic activity millions of years ago, whereas everyone knows that the Irish giant Fionn mac Cumhaill (Finn MacCool) built the Causeway so that he could walk to Scotland to confront his counterpart Benandonner.
(Trevor James Hunter/fotoLibra/443760)

FAR RIGHT: Crab and lobster pots ready to be dropped into the Atlantic from fishing boats based in the busy little fishing village of Ballyvaughan, County Clare. Note The Burren in the background, on the northern side of Galway Bay.
(Cherry Dian Spooner/fotoLibra/496210)

OVER PAGE: Rising close to the Atlantic near the northwest coast of Ireland, Mount Errigal (right) is the highest peak (at about 2,500 feet) in the Derrveagh Mountains of north Donegal, while the flat-topped Muckish is the third highest at 2,185 feet.
(The Irish Image Collection/Corbis/42-19013708)

Hills and Mountains

Hills and Mountains

Some of the most spectacular views of Ireland are of and from hills and mountains. Ireland is not particularly mountainous in terms of height, but there are almost fifty mountain ranges, and more than fifty individual peaks, the highest of which is Carrauntoohil, County Kerry, at about 3,415 feet. There are only three peaks higher than 3,280 feet, while about 455 are higher than 1,640 feet. The center section of Ireland, known as the Midlands, is a mostly flat, low-lying area surrounded by mountain ranges, while some ranges are farther inland in the south. These include the Galtee Mountains, the highest inland range.

Attractions that bring thousands of tourists to Ireland each year include rambling and hill walking. To get the most enjoyment out of such activities it is recommended that participants join an organized club whose members include leaders with great knowledge of specific areas and experience of the pleasures and difficulties associated with them. One such club is the Irish Ramblers Club, which grades walks according to the difficulty of the terrain and the level of fitness required to complete them, and provides a lot of useful information on a particular walk as well as rambling/walking in general. Walkers in Ireland may start in forest tracks, but can expect to spend most of the time on rough terrain or on boggy ground, and the club will be able to advise on what to take on a trip, such as items of clothing, emergency rations, and first aid kit.

RIGHT: For several hundred years before the eleventh century Norman invasion, the hilltop fortress complex on the Rock of Cashel, in County Tipperary, was the traditional seat of the kings of Munster, and boasts the remnants of one of the finest collections of Celtic and medieval architecture in Europe.
(Andy Jay/fotoLibra/149520)

FAR RIGHT: The highest peak in Ireland, at about 3,400 feet, is County Kerry's Mount Carrauntoohil (farthest peak to the left), seen from a valley bog. While steep in parts, it is not a difficult climb for the properly equipped.
(Deanna Witzel/iStockphoto/3937272)

FAR LEFT: Superb trout and salmon fishing are to be enjoyed on Lough Conn, which spreads across 14,000 acres in County Mayo, beneath Mount Nephin, at 2,645 feet the second highest peak in the county (after Mweelrea).
(Daemys/iStockphoto/3839559)

LEFT: County Wicklow boasts three "Sugar Loaf" mountains: the Sugar Loaf in the west of the county, and the Great Sugar Loaf and Little Sugar Loaf in the east.
(Caitriona Dwyer/iStockphoto/1256119)

RIGHT: A view of Mount Brandon from Conor Pass, County Kerry. Its craggy appearance is the result of glacial scraping on the east side during the Ice Age, while its west side escaped that activity, and its summit is rounded and smooth.
(Michael Walsh/iStockphoto/7387574)

FAR RIGHT: The Ring of Kerry, in the southwest, is undoubtedly beautiful, and its attractions—outstanding scenery, quaint villages, fabulous sandy beaches, fishing, watersports, cycling, walking, and horse-riding—draw the crowds in their thousands, begging the question as to whether the tranquillity of this mystical and relatively unspoilt region suffers during high season.
(Joe Gough/iStockphoto/5157988)

RIGHT: The magnificent scenery in the hills of Westport, County Mayo, ensures that the region is a major tourist destination, particularly for those who enjoy sea-angling and freshwater fishing, and strenuous hill-walking.
(Jonathan Barton/iStockphoto/7921661)

FAR RIGHT: O'Brien's Tower was built on the Cliffs of Moher in 1835 by local landlord Sir Cornelius O'Brien to serve and attract tourists as a boost to the economy of the region. It stands proudly on a headland of the majestic cliffs, from where can be seen the Aran Islands, Galway Bay, The Twelve Pins, the Maum Turk Mountains in Connemara, and Loop Head to the south.
(Tito Slack/iStockphoto/1057194)

OVER PAGE: Mulroy Bay, just outside the small town of Milford, County Donegal, is a sea loch about twelve miles long, running north to south and opening to the Atlantic Ocean. Caution is required when navigating the loch, mainly because of the many small, rocky islands and islets.
(Brendan Montgomery/fotoLibra/495803)

Rivers and Lakes

Rivers and Lakes

Ireland is bisected by the River Shannon, which flows roughly from north to south, separating the west of Ireland (mainly the province of Connacht) from the east and south (Leinster and most of Munster). At 240 miles long, the Shannon is the longest river in Ireland, flowing south from Shannon Pot, in County Cavan, and then turning west to the Atlantic via the seventy-mile-long Shannon Estuary. There are fewer than twenty crossing points between Limerick City in the south and the village of Dowra in the north. There are several canal connections with the Shannon, used by tourists and commercial haulage traffic. In all there are about seventy-five rivers flowing through the Republic and Northern Ireland.

Lakes in Ireland are usually called "loughs," and there are at least fifty in the Republic and Northern Ireland of some geographic, geological, or historical significance, plus many other minor bodies of water. Lough Neagh in Northern Ireland is the largest lake in Great Britain and Ireland. Most of the lakes are either freshwater or brackish, but Lady's Island Lake in County Wexford is neither fresh nor salt water since it has no outlet: it is separated from the Atlantic by a 670-foot-long sand and gravel bar through which salt water seeps, while fresh water runs into the lake from the surrounding land.

Among the major attractions Ireland has to offer are salmon and trout angling on the rivers and lakes, and also boat fishing and surfcasting around the coastline. There are certainly still many places where anglers can find the unique combination of superb sport and quietude in beautiful locations.

RIGHT: In Ennistymon, a small town in County Clare, two miles inland from the Atlantic, the River Cullenagh runs fast in small rapids behind the main street and forms a beautiful cascade about a mile-and-a-half away from where it joins the River Derry. These two rivers continue toward the sea as the Inagh River.
(Vernon Parker/fotoLibra/444991)

FAR RIGHT: The waters of the Shannon, at 240 miles Ireland's longest river, surface from the Shannon Pot in County Cavan and flow through ten of Ireland's counties into the Atlantic near Limerick City. Upstream, on the east bank (at right in the photo), can be seen King John's Castle, completed at Limerick around the year 1200.
(David Rubinton/iStockphoto/4934169)

FAR LEFT: The ruins of Cloughoughter Castle in Lough Oughter, County Cavan, a complex of lakes on the River Erne forming the southern part of the Lough Erne complex. The Erne in Northern Ireland is linked to the Shannon in the Republic of Ireland by the Shannon/Erne Waterway.
(The Irish Image Collection/Corbis/42-19009598)

LEFT: Doo Lough, a beautiful lake of some 220 acres, and Sheefry Hills, County Mayo. The lake is a long sheet of water with mountains rising steeply on all sides. The views are particularly splendid at sunset.
(The Irish Image Collection/Corbis/42-19013079)

OVER PAGE: It is astonishing to learn that in the eleventh century the small County Clare town of Killaloe (with a current population of fewer than fifteen hundred people) was the most important place in all Ireland. Apparently it was from here that High King Brian Boru, who had his palace (Kincora) where the current Catholic church stands and his fort just north of the town, could command the strategic crossing of the River Shannon above Limerick, where the Vikings were in control.
(Vernon Parker/fotoLibra/447616)

RIGHT: Fishing for salmon and trout couldn't be more enjoyable than here, on the small, romantic lake of Gougane Barra in County Cork. Nestled in the Derrynesaggart Mountains, it is the source of the River Lee. In the middle of the lake, reached by a causeway, is an island on which is the site of the sixth century hermitage of St. Finbarr, founder and first Bishop of Cork. The ruins seen today, however, are from the seventeenth century.
(Philippa Wood/fotoLibra/495624)

FAR RIGHT: To complete the famed Ring of Kerry tourist drive one must pass through the small County Kerry town of Sneem, just as the river of that name does.
(Robert Harding World Imagery/Corbis/ 42-18638379)

LEFT: Waterskiing past Castle Island on the almost circular Lough Key, a lake located to the northeast of Boyle, County Roscommon. There are over thirty wooded islands on the lake; this one boasts Macdermott's Castle, named after one of the most important families in the district.
(The Irish Image Collection/Corbis/42-19019495)

RIGHT: The ruins of a monk's fishing cottage on the River Cong, County Mayo. The river is the outflow of Lough Mask, where the waters escape through massive fissures in the cavernous limestone, and rise again in the village of Cong (famous for the filming there of John Ford's 1952 Oscar-winning film, *The Quiet Man*, starring John Wayne). (Meldayus/iStockphoto/859558)

FAR RIGHT: In County Kerry, the River Laune flows from Lough Leane (one of the Killarney lakes), through the town of Killorglin (seen here, famous for its annual Puck Fair, the oldest traditional fair in Ireland), and thence to the sea at Castlemaine Harbor and Dingle Bay. (Paul Thompson/Corbis/42-19069700)

OVER PAGE: Office buildings and the cityscape of Dublin at twilight are reflected in the River Liffey, which divides the Northside of the city from the Southside. For many centuries up to modern times the Liffey was used for trade, but in recent years the only regular traffic on the river within the city has been the Liffey Voyage water tour bus service, which runs guided tours along the river through Dublin City center. The city is connected to the River Shannon via the Grand Canal and the Royal Canal. (The Irish Image Collection/Corbis/42-19011498)

Towns and Cities

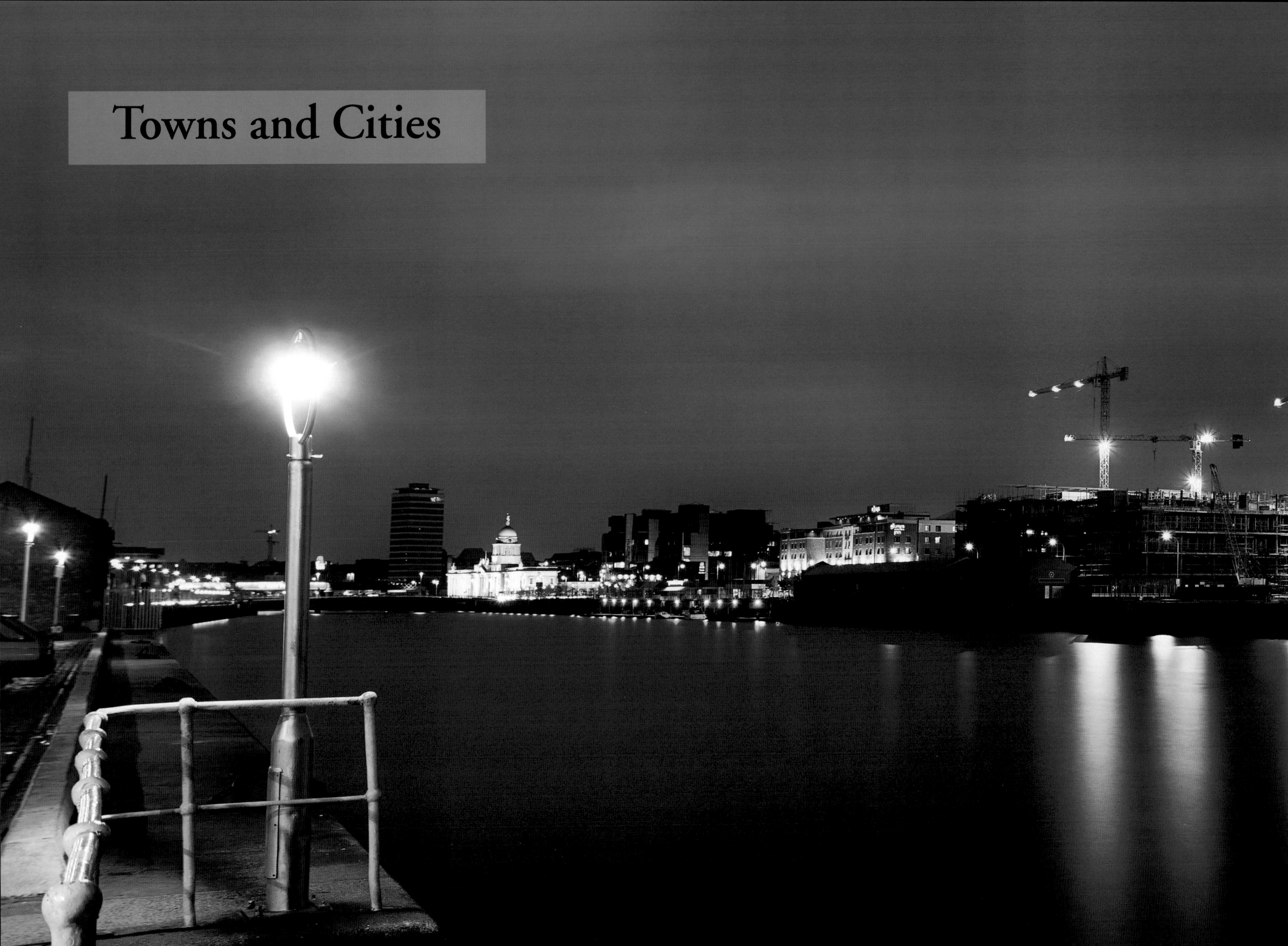

Towns and Cities

In the Republic of Ireland there are five "official" cities (Dublin, Cork, Galway, Limerick, and Waterford), all of which trace their status to historic royal charters. A sixth, Kilkenny, legally a town, is permitted to use the title for ceremonial purposes. There are also five official cities in Northern Ireland (Armagh, Belfast, Derry, Lisburn, and Newry), while what is now Downpatrick, County Down, was formerly recognized as the "City of Down" but its city status was not maintained from the seventeenth century.

Dublin is both the largest city in the Republic and its capital. The River Liffey divides the city in two: the Northside, by tradition representing the working class, and the Southside the middle and upper middle classes. Its population (in the city) is in excess of 506,000, while the total population of the Greater Dublin Area is about 1.66 million. The economic boom years of the 1990s and early 2000s saw a surge in construction, but Dublin has suffered from the general economic downturn, and unemployment figures have increased, while city development plans may also be affected.

Belfast is the capital city of Northern Ireland, with a population of over 275,000 in the city proper, while to this can be added the 800,000 of the Belfast Regional Area. Quite apart from the economic problems that Belfast (and the rest of the world) has, the city also bore the brunt of the sectarian violence (commonly referred to as the "Troubles"), particularly during the last quarter of the twentieth century. However, a cessation of day-to-day violence has led to greater investor confidence, and an increase in tourism, which hopefully will lead to much-needed city redevelopment.

RIGHT: One of Ireland's most famous buildings, the General Post Office (GPO) is sited in the center of Dublin's main thoroughfare, O'Connell Street. In 1916 leaders of the failed "Easter Rising" used the GPO as their headquarters, and it was extensively damaged by British forces who assaulted the building, Bullet marks can still be seen on the original columns outside, and the building remains a symbol of Irish nationalism. (Nigel Coates/fotoLibra/495917)

FAR RIGHT: Prior to 1816 when Dublin's Ha'penny Bridge was built over the River Liffey, there were seven dilapidated ferries operated by William Walsh, who was ordered to repair the ferries or build a pedestrian bridge. He chose the latter, and was permitted to charge a toll of a ha'penny (half a penny). The toll was dropped in 1919. (Marek Slusarczyk/iStockphoto/4799416)

RIGHT: The sun's reflection gleams off the side of an office block in Belfast city center. The site has been occupied since the Bronze Age, becoming a substantial settlement in the seventeenth century, and growing as a commercial and industrial center for the next two hundred years. Belfast has been the capital of Northern Ireland since its establishment in 1921.
(Jonathan Maddock/iStockphoto/5521207)

FAR RIGHT: Customs House, one of Belfast's finest architectural features, was designed by Charles Lanyon in 1857, and built on Donegall Quay. At right of center is the thirty-three-foot Big Fish, a printed ceramic mosaic sculpture constructed in 1999 by John Kindness.
(Alan McCabe/fotoLibra/495743)

FAR LEFT: Queen Victoria granted Belfast city status in 1888 and ten years later construction began for the building of the City Hall, which was completed in 1906. Covering an acre and a half, with an enclosed courtyard, the building is in the "Classical Renaissance" style featuring green copper-coated domes at each of the four corners and a lantern-crowned brass dome in the center.
(Brendan Montgomery/fotoLibra/366541)

LEFT: The Spiral Bridge over the Belfast to Bangor railway line operated by Northern Ireland Railways, at Ballymacarrett Halt, which opened in May 1905 and closed in May 1977.
(Robert McEvoy/fotoLibra/15173)

LEFT: With the tide out you can almost smell the mud and hear the swooping gulls in the deep natural harbor of Bantry, County Cork. Beneath a dull, early morning sky, this scene would be drab indeed were it not for the colorful houses at the waterfront. Bantry, along with many other areas on the southwest coast, claims a connection with the sixth century saint, Breandán, who, according to Irish folklore, discovered America.
(Stuart Henry Neesham/fotoLibra/496058)

RIGHT: Colorful shops and eateries in a pedestrianized area welcome tourists to the historic town of Kinsale in County Cork. During the summer months, at the height of the holiday season, Kinsale's population of about 2,250 swells many times over.
(The Irish Image Collection/Corbis/42-19008278)

FAR RIGHT: Glandore is an attractive village on the east side of the harbor of the same name in County Cork. It and the surrounding area are extremely popular with the summer vacation boating fraternity. On the west side is Union Hall, and the two villages are frequently referred to together. Union Hall has a thriving fishing fleet, and is a base for whale- and dolphin-watching.
(The Irish Image Collection/Corbis/42-19010127)

FAR LEFT: Kilkenny, in the center of County Kilkenny in southeast Ireland, sits on both banks of the River Nore. It is the smallest city in the Republic of Ireland, and also the only city in Ireland that is not tidal. Its status as a city was granted by royal charter in 1609 by King James I of England. (The Irish Image Collection/Corbis/42-19014016)

LEFT: More than sixty fishing boats may be counted in Killybegs harbor at any one time, reflecting this County Donegal town's main commercial activity. Indeed, it lays claim to being the most productive fishing port in all Ireland. A downside is that, with the port having its own fish processing plants, effluent expelled from the factories can be smelled for miles around. In addition, the harbor handles many other types of shipping, including passenger cruise liners and cargo vessels. (The Irish Image Collection/Corbis/42-19019423)

RIGHT: The three spires of the Church of Ireland's St. Fin Barre's Cathedral tower above Cork, the second largest city (after Dublin) in the Republic of Ireland, on the River Lee. The deep harbor permits ships of any size to enter, enhancing the city's commerce. Many famous trading names are linked to Cork, including the brewers of Murphy's and Beamish (Heineken), while the local pharmaceutical industry's most famous product is sildenafil citrate, sold as Viagra.
(Colin William Turner/fotoLibra/495786)

STATION MASTER'S OFFICE

FAR LEFT: The popular café in the restored railway station of Cobh, County Cork, one of the few towns outside the Dublin metropolitan area served by a commuter train service. It is effectively the southern terminus of the railway line from Dublin to Cork. The station is just one of the visible improvements to amenities made in recent years, for the benefit of local inhabitants as well as tourists visiting the east coast.
(The Irish Image Collection/Corbis/42-19010927)

LEFT: World famous for its 200-year-old glass and crystal making industry, the city of Waterford, in County Waterford, was established by the Vikings in the early tenth century. The River Suir flows through the city, which for a thousand years has been one of Ireland's most important ports.
(Richard Cummins/Corbis/ CU942664)

OVER PAGE: Originally built between 1863 and 1868 as a private residence in Connemara, County Galway (and at that time called Kylemore Castle), Kylemore Abbey became a Benedictine monastery in 1920, founded by nuns who fled Belgium during the First World War (1914–1918). The grounds house a neo-Gothic church built between 1877 and 1881, a miniature replica of Norwich Cathedral, and a Victorian walled garden.
(Geray Sweeney/Corbis/AABS001090)

Places of Worship

Places of Worship

There are certainly no shortages of buildings and sites that have been or still are places of worship in Ireland, They include beautiful cathedrals, derelict but historic churches, abbeys and monasteries, and ancient tombs and burial grounds. Worshippers from all eras since the Stone Age have left their marks above and below ground deemed sacred, where they have participated in ritual burials, thanksgivings, and other religious services. There are few remains of the Viking era still intact, although one feature almost exclusive to Ireland is the round tower, usually built within a monastery as a place of refuge or lookout post during Viking raids. There were a considerable number of churches built in medieval Ireland, and thankfully some (or parts of them) still exist as a result of restoration.

During the twelfth and thirteenth centuries the Normans were the main influence on church design, bringing to Ireland the Gothic style, as seen in Christ Church and St. Patrick's Cathedral in Dublin. Such medieval influences from Britain and mainland Europe persisted for centuries, even being revived as neo-Gothic styles (such as Lancet arched Gothic) in the eighteenth century, in contrast to the classical and Romanticism styles prevalent at the time.

As has been the case for hundreds of years, the dominant religion in the Republic of Ireland is Roman Catholicism with upwards of 3,680,000 adherents out of a total of about 4,240,000 (according to the 2006 census). The next strongest (numerically) is the Church of Ireland, with 126,000 worshippers. There are almost 680,000 Roman Catholic adherents in Northern Ireland, almost 350,000 people who belong to the Presbyterian Church, and nearly 260,000 worshippers with the Church of Ireland.

RIGHT: Muckross Abbey in Killarney National Park, County Kerry, was founded in 1448 by Donal McCarthy, chieftain of Desmond, as a Franciscan Friary for the Observantine Franciscans. Throughout the next two hundred years the abbey was the target of much violence from various marauders and had to undergo significant repairs and rebuilding until it was finally abandoned in about 1652. (Tom Bean/Corbis/7789724)

FAR RIGHT: Such is the continuing interest in the Drombeg stone circle (Drom Beag meaning "little hillock"), located about a mile-and-a-half east of Glandore, County Cork, that the area has been covered in gravel to protect it from the volume of visitors. Thirteen of the original seventeen stones survive. The circle measures twenty-nine feet in diameter, and the stones, which were positioned well before the fifth and sixth centuries, are oriented toward the setting sun during the midwinter solstice. (Joe Gough/iStockphoto/4144031)

FAR LEFT: The entrance to an ancient tomb on a famous prehistoric site called Brú na Bóinne in County Meath. Constructed nearly 5,000 years ago overlooking the River Boyne, the site is about 330 feet in diameter and 50 feet in height. A long passageway from this opening leads to the cruciform-shaped center of the mound. For about seven days around winter solstice, a narrow beam of sunlight shines onto the floor through the upper chamber visible here. The rock in the front shows an intricate mosaic, although its meaning isn't clear. (Stephan Hoerold/iStockphoto/6879703)

LEFT: The ruins of Jerpoint Abbey, a Cistercian abbey near Thomastown, County Kilkenny, founded between 1163 and 1165 by Donal MacGillapatrick I, King of Ossory. The Romanesque architecture, particularly in the eastern arm, is notable for its stone carvings. (Brian Kelly/iStockphoto/465753)

RIGHT: Dublin has two medieval cathedrals, St. Patrick's and this one, Christ Church, which is officially claimed as the seat of both the Church of Ireland and Roman Catholic archbishops of Dublin. Road development, including the laying of a dual carriageway (highway), means that the cathedral now appears isolated, away from its original medieval context.
(Nigel B. Coates/fotoLibra/495901)

FAR RIGHT: It is reputed that St. Patrick brought Christianity to Ireland early in the fifth century, and that when he died his remains were buried at the site where the Church of Ireland Down Cathedral in Downpatrick, County Down, stands on the site of a Benedictine monastery built in 1183. A memorial stone, a slab of granite from the nearby Mourne Mountains, was put in position by the Belfast Naturalists' Field Club in 1900 to mark his grave.
(John Lees/fotoLibra/495292)

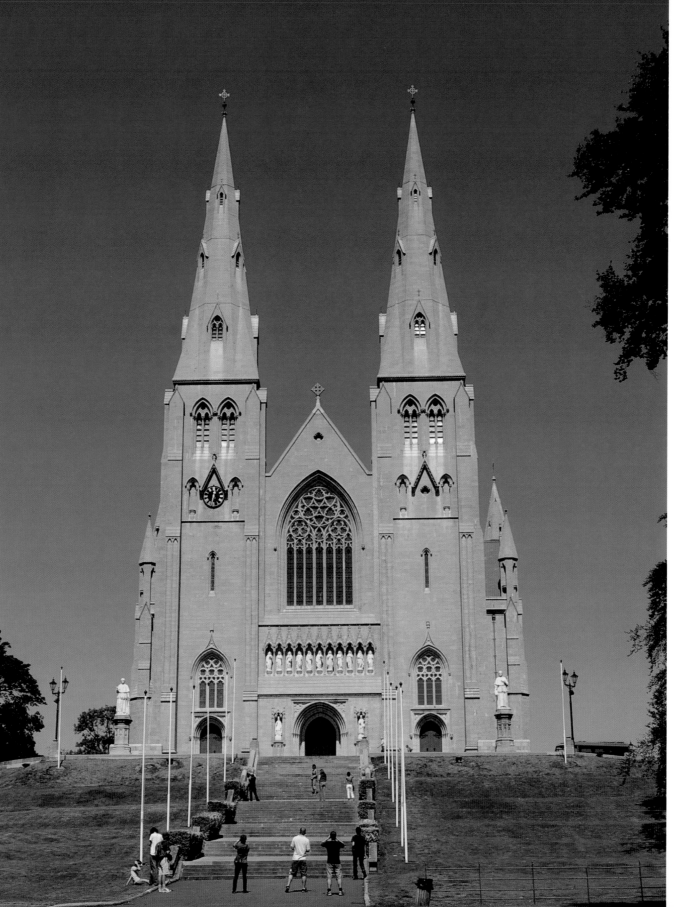

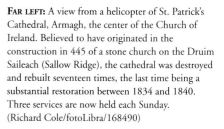

FAR LEFT: A view from a helicopter of St. Patrick's Cathedral, Armagh, the center of the Church of Ireland. Believed to have originated in the construction in 445 of a stone church on the Druim Saileach (Sallow Ridge), the cathedral was destroyed and rebuilt seventeen times, the last time being a substantial restoration between 1834 and 1840. Three services are now held each Sunday.
(Richard Cole/fotoLibra/168490)

LEFT: Armagh, in County Armagh, is the only city in the world to have two cathedrals with the same name, St. Patrick's. This Roman Catholic cathedral was built in the 1800s. Its twin spires, at over 200 feet, stand taller than any other structures in the county.
(Brendan Montgomery/fotoLibra/164798)

FAR LEFT: Clonmacnois, beside the River Shannon in County Offaly, is one of the most important monastic sites in Ireland, boasting the ruins of eight churches, a cathedral, two round towers, five high crosses, more than 200 slabs from graves, and the remains of a fortified tower—all the focus of an annual pilgrimage on September 9, and one of the places visited by Pope John Paul in 1979. (Nicola Keegan/iStockphoto/5528968)

LEFT: St. Mary's is a Roman Catholic cathedral in Killarney, County Kerry. Among its most notable features are its pointed style, known as Lancet and Gothic, its long, slender Lancet windows, and its acutely pointed arches. Financial constraints protracted and interrupted the cathedral's construction, so that it took twenty-seven years from original concept to consecration, which occurred on August 22, 1855. (Rolf Weschke/iStockphoto/1878876)

RIGHT: St. Canice's Cathedral in County Kilkenny stands to the northeast of the town on a site that has been used for Christian worship since the sixth century. It was built in the thirteenth century, and beside it is a ninth century round tower, which is believed to have been a watchtower overlooking the town of Kilkenny and surrounding countryside. (Andrea Jemolo/Corbis/AJ001886)

FAR RIGHT: St. Canice was a monk and missionary who was born about 515 at Glengiven, County Derry, was ordained in Wales, visited Rome, and then preached in Ireland before traveling to Scotland. The graceful cathedral established in his name has been preserved in its original style and form. It is richly endowed with many stained glass windows and some of the finest sixteenth century monuments. (Stephen Power/fotoLibra/495237)

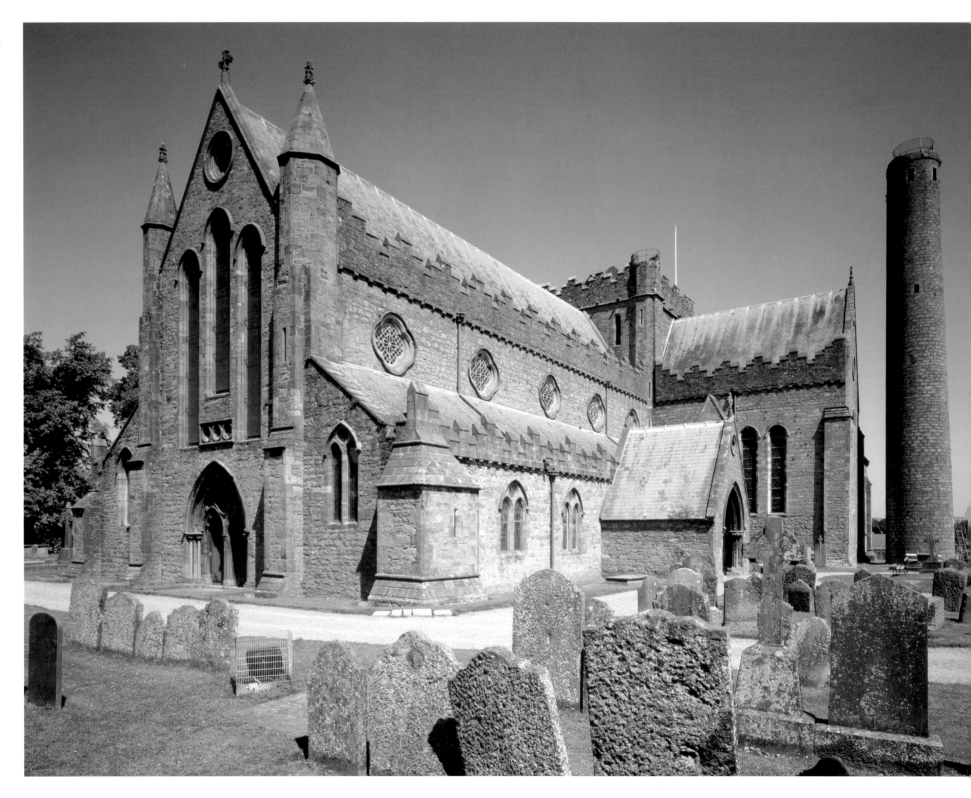

FAR LEFT: A twilight view of the cathedral at the Rock of Cashel in County Tipperary, one of the most important historical sites in Ireland. The thirteenth century Gothic-style cathedral is the largest surviving building on the Rock. (Richard Cummins/Corbis/ CU942141)

LEFT: St. Columb's Cathedral, Londonderry, as seen from Church Bastion, a canon emplacement on the siege wall that surrounds the city. It dates from 1633, and in its porch there is the following inscription: "If stones could speake then London's prayse should sound/Who built this church and cittie from the grounde." (Roger Bradley/iStockphoto/6476045)

ABOVE: The monastery at Glendalough in County Wicklow was established by St. Kevin who, according to legend, lived to the age of 120 years (from 498 to 618), throughout which he became known for his disdain of human company, particularly that of women. (Bertrand Rieger/Hemis/Corbis/42-19834693)

Left: Across the River Shannon at Killaloe, County Clare, is St. Flannan's Cathedral, built between 1185 and 1225, and destroyed and rebuilt in the fourteenth century.
(The Irish Image Collection/Corbis/42-19018710)

Over page: Enniskillen Castle, situated beside the River Erne in County Fermanagh, was built almost 600 years ago by Gaelic Maguire chieftains. Guarding one of the few passes into Ulster, it was strategically important throughout its history. In the seventeenth century it became an English garrison fort and later served as part of a military barracks.
(Brendan Montogomery/fotoLibra/495426)

Castles and Fortifications

Castles and Fortifications

On Inishmore, the largest of the Aran Islands, situated on a cliff some three hundred feet high, is the great "fortress" of Dún Aonghusa (Dún Aengus). No one knows for sure what its purpose was, or even who built it (very probably Celtic settlers, for their protection against frequent raiders). There are the remains of several other such prehistoric forts in the islands and elsewhere in Ireland. Such huge fortifications gave way to smaller, often temporary constructions, built in wood and later in stone, for defense against Viking raiders.

Today, there are more than 380 "castles" in Ireland, the vast majority of them (about 325) in the Republic. Some of these "castles" are now not much more than parts of crumbling walls, whereas others have been painstakingly restored and are now open as tourist attractions or as hotels, or even as private residences. The high point of castle building was during the thirteenth century Norman period, when three-quarters of Ireland was under Norman control. This was the time when some magnificent stone castles were erected in the best strategic positions overlooking important rivers and towns.

Common features of castles of the period were a central main tower, or keep, high walls around the keep, several additional walls that often enclosed courtyards, thick external walls, moats, drawbridges and gatehouses. The walls contained arrow slits, and at the top of a castle were battlements or ramparts providing cover from which defending soldiers could fire arrows or use other weapons against besieging forces. Building stone castles frequently took decades, and used a great deal of manpower, especially cheap labor. Religion was an important part of medieval life, and so churches or chapels were often included in castles and other fortifications.

Many of the castles built in the medieval period were very large structures, reflecting the enormous wealth and power of the Anglo-Norman barons. Later, from about 1400 to 1640, smaller tower houses were erected by the landed gentry for their protection. However, by the time of the 1641 Rebellion, artillery was in widespread use, and such fortresses could be surrounded and bombarded into submission.

ABOVE: The massive semicircular ruins of the Dún Aengus ringfort, close to the edge of 300-foot cliffs on the southern coast of the island of Inishmore, one of the Aran Islands, comprise three concentric enclosures; the walls of the inner citadel alone were twenty feet high and eighteen feet wide. The ruins date from between the first century B.C. and the Late Bronze Age, around 700 B.C (Michael St. Maur Sheil/Corbis/SH001246)

RIGHT: In all, Dún Aengus stretches for fourteen acres. It is not known whether the fort was more important for religious ritual rather than for military defense. It is most likely that it was constructed by a group of people who had retreated from the mainland to the Aran Islands and felt themselves threatened. (Michael St. Maur Sheil/Corbis/SH001242)

FAR RIGHT: Probably the best known monument in Inishowen, County Donegal, and situated on a hilltop 800 feet above sea level, Grianan of Aileach is a circular fort believed to have been originally built as a pagan temple about the fifth century B.C. Different views have been expressed as to whether it was a defensive or ceremonial site. (Eye Ubiquitous/Corbis/UB881953)

FAR LEFT: The largest castle in Ireland, and the largest Norman castle in Europe, Trim Castle in County Meath dates from the end of the twelfth century, when it was built on raised ground overlooking a fording point over the River Boyne. In 1994/1995 it was used by actor/director/producer Mel Gibson in the filming of his award-winning movie *Braveheart*.
(Paul Mcnamara/fotoLibta/395016)

LEFT: Carrickfergus Castle in Carrickfergus, County Antrim, is on the edge of Belfast Lough. It played an important military role for some 750 years, right up to 1928, when the government took ownership for preservation as an ancient monument. The castle was a key to the Anglo-Norman hold on Ulster in the late twelfth and early thirteenth centuries, while several centuries later, during the American Revolutionary War, John Paul Jones won an hour-long battle against a Royal Navy warship that was lured from its moorings in Carrickfergus into the North Channel of the Irish Sea.
(Roger Bradley/iStockphoto/6412126)

RIGHT: Dunluce Castle, in County Antrim, is sited dramatically close to the edge of a headland, along the North Antrim coast. Surrounded by fabulous coastal scenery, this medieval castle stands where an early Irish fort was once built and where its history can be traced back to early Christians and Vikings. Terrifyingly steep drops surround the castle, which is connected to the mainland via a bridge.
(John Lennon/fotoLibra/155535)

FAR RIGHT: The village of Hillsborough, County Down, takes its name from Sir Arthur Hill, who built the 270-foot-square Hillsborough Fort on rising ground in 1650 to command the road from Dublin to Belfast and Carrickfergus. The Hill family became the Earls of Hillsborough, then Marquises of Downshire.
(The Irish Image Collection/Corbis/42-19784291)

RIGHT: King John's Castle, Limerick, is situated on King's Island, on the southern bank of the River Shannon, next to Thomond Bridge. It was built by the Anglo-Normans between 1200 and 1210, although the site had previously seen much conflict, especially while under the control of the Vikings, who used it as a base from which to raid up and down the river.
(Agitons/iStockphoto/2335573)

FAR RIGHT: The walls of King John's Castle were severely damaged in the Siege of Limerick in 1642, the first of five sieges of the city in the seventeenth century. Many repairs and extensions took place during the following centuries.
(Stephen Power/fotoLibra/495250)

LEFT: The first stone castle to be built on this site in Kilkenny was square-shaped with towers at each corner. It was completed in 1213, and three of the towers have survived. Formerly privately owned by the Butler family from 1391, the castle was given to the nation in 1967.
(Noel Mealy/fotoLibra/495201)

RIGHT: Dunguaire Castle, a sixteenth century tower house, is positioned on rising ground on the southeastern shore of Galway Bay, County Galway, just outside the tiny village of Kinvara. It has many claims to fame, among them being that it is "the most photographed castle in Ireland." The tower and other parts have been successfully restored, and the castle and grounds are a major attraction to tourists during the summer months.
(Tito Slack/iStockphoto/1073546)

FAR RIGHT: Johnstown Castle and its fifty-acre grounds in County Wexford are a major draw for tourists. Visitors will be delighted to stroll through wooded grounds, relax by the lakeside, sit and watch the dazzling birdlife, and visit the Irish Agricultural Museum within the grounds. But they will be disappointed that the picturesque castle is not open to the public.
(Doorly/iStockphoto/5704319)

RIGHT: Reginald's Tower, in Waterford, was named after the early eleventh century Viking chief Ragnvald. The circular tower, part of the town's defenses, was built early in the thirteenth century, with a second phase in the fifteenth. It has since been used as a mint, a munitions store, and a prison. Restored, it now houses the city museum. (K. Stuart/Brian Kelly/iStockphoto/140890)

FAR RIGHT: Cahir Castle, County Tipperary, one of the largest castles in Ireland, was built in the twelfth century by Conor O'Brien, the Lord of Thomond, on a stony outcrop island in the River Suir. It was around this focal point that the town of Cahir developed. Some parts of the original castle became incorporated in the later strong and imposing Anglo-Norman castle, built in the fifteenth/sixteenth centuries. (Rognar/iStockphoto/3223206)

FAR LEFT: The main monument in the group named Grianan of Aileach, in County Donegal, is this Iron Age stone ringfort whose internal diameter is over 75 feet and whose walls are about 16 feet high and 13 feet thick.
(Mark Fearon/fotoLibra/495360)

LEFT: The origins of the Grianan of Aileach ringfort date back to 1700 B.C., while the structure seen today is the result of extensive restoration in the 1870s.
(Mark Fearon/fotoLibra/495358)

ABOVE: Birr Castle in County Offaly is famous for its contribution to science, and in particular for the 72-inch telescope built there during the 1840s. It was created from scratch by the third Earl of Rosse, who designed and had built the mirrors, tube, and mountings, and assembled what was at the time the largest telescope in the world.
(Mark Stokes/iStockphoto/101212)

FAR LEFT: Malahide Castle is set in 250 acres of parkland in the seaside town of Malahide, about ten miles north of Dublin City. It has been both a fortress and a private home for almost 800 years, having been the residence of the Talbot family from 1185 to 1973.
(UnaPhoto/iStockphoto/7470331)

LEFT: Ross Castle, on the edge of Lough Leane in Killarney National Park, County Kerry, is a typical stronghold of an Irish chieftain during the Middle Ages. It was probably built in the late fifteenth century by one of the O'Donoghue Ross chieftains. It is surrounded by a fortified bawn (the defensive wall surrounding an Irish tower house, to protect livestock during an attack), its curtain walls defended by circular flanking towers, two of which remain. Much of the bawn was removed by the time the barrack building was added on the south side of the castle in the middle of the eighteenth century.
(afj1977/iStockphoto/6984761)

OVER PAGE: The avenue leading to the Palladian-style Powerscourt House, at Enniskerry, County Wicklow, is a mile long and is lined by over 2,000 beech trees. The house that we see today was built in the eighteenth century around the shell of a fourteenth century castle. It was gutted by fire in 1974, but was restored and is now a very popular tourist destination.
(Eye Ubiquitous/Corbis/ UB881950)

Historic Houses

Visitors to Ireland are especially drawn to the very many "historic houses," parts or the whole of which, together with their gardens, are open to the general public. We are using this term rather loosely here, rather than in the strict sense. The houses can be "stately homes" that are being lovingly maintained at high personal cost to the incumbent or the relevant "department of public works." Or they could be great country mansions of the landed gentry, perhaps with beautifully landscaped and maintained gardens and grounds. Unofficially, the term "historic houses" can also be used to describe such stately homes that are now serving as luxury hotels "for discerning travelers," or as museums. Historic houses may be those whose claim to fame may merely be that they were the birthplaces of famous individuals, or have been designed in a significant architectural style.

Some of the houses featured in the following pages fit neatly into the above categories, while there are others that have been selected because they are representative of a style, or a period, or a specific purpose—see pages 136 (Mansion House), 138 (the brightly painted village house), and 139 (farm cottage) for examples.

There are many "historic" houses that could not be included, because of space constraints, one being the "market house." This was a notable house in the center of a market town, featuring various architectural styles, sizes and ornamentation. At ground level there were three, four or five bays forming an arcade, while an upper floor may have been used as a courthouse or ballroom. Ornamentation would have been a dome, a tower, a clock, or a cupola. While many of these market houses are now derelict, there are others that now serve as cultural venues or business premises.

RIGHT: Powerscourt House near Enniskerry, County Wicklow, sits in forty-seven acres of magnificent gardens and grounds. To the north, formal tree plantations were laid to frame the vista from the house, while to the south were created a formal Italian garden, a walled garden, fish pond, cascades, grottoes, and terraces. (The Irish Image Collection/Corbis/42-19010702)

FAR RIGHT: Russborough House in Blessington, County Kildare, was designed by renowned German architect Richard Cassells (anglicized to Castle) and built in local granite in 1741. It is in the Palladian style, with a central block with colonnades and two wings. The front façade of the house has a fine flight of steps, with heraldic lions and urns, a sweep of graceful curved colonnades crowned on the skyline with baroque urns, and well-proportioned, solid flanking wings. (The Irish Image Collection/Corbis/42-19009192)

LEFT: Bantry House, in Bantry, County Cork, was built in about 1700 on the south side of Bantry Bay, and therefore benefits from magnificent views. It was originally called "Blackrock House" by previous owners, but the name was changed to "Seafield" by the prosperous family headed by Councillor Richard White, who became Baron Bantry in 1797, hence the further change of name. The house and beautiful gardens have remained in Bantry family ownership ever since.
(The Irish Image Collection/Corbis/42-19015999)

FAR LEFT: Dating from the seventeenth century, Killruddery House is surrounded by picturesque formal gardens in Bray, County Wicklow. It has been the location for several internationally successful movies, including *Lassie*, *The Tudors*, *My Left Foot*, and *Becoming Jane*.
(The Irish Image Collection/Corbis/42-19010752)

LEFT: The lakeside façade of Westport House, County Mayo. The present owners, the Browne family, are direct descendants of the sixteenth century "Pirate Queen" Grace O'Malley or Granuaile. She had several castles in the west of Ireland and it was on the foundations of one of these that Westport House was built.
(Hugh Rooney; Eye Ubiquitous/Corbis/UB005107)

RIGHT: Adare Manor is a nineteenth century manor house located on the banks of the River Maigue in the village of Adare, County Limerick. It is now a luxury hotel and golf resort, with an 840-acre estate on which is an eighteen-hole championship golf course that has become home to the Irish Open competition.
(Robert Simon/iStockphoto/6134686)

FAR RIGHT: The north rear façade of Áras an Uachtaráin. Formerly the Viceregal Lodge, it is the official residence of the president of Ireland, located in Phoenix Park on the Northside of Dublin. Its construction began in 1780 but, when completed, it stood empty for several years until the office of president was created in 1937.
(Nigel B. Coates/fotoLibra/444372)

FAR LEFT: Castletown House, Celbridge, County Kildare, is Ireland's largest and earliest Palladian-style house, built between 1722 and 1729 for William Conolly, Speaker of the Irish House of Commons, and at the time the wealthiest commoner in Ireland. In 1994 the house, with the exception of the contents, was transferred to State care, paving the way for a major program of restoration and conservation work of the house and demesne lands. (The Irish Image Collection/Corbis/42-19019762)

LEFT: Castle Ward, overlooking Strangford Lough, Downpatrick, County Down, is an interesting eighteenth century mansion displaying a mixture of architectural styles, including a Classical and a Gothic façade.
(The Irish Image Collection/Corbis 42-19007444)

RIGHT: Mansion House is located on Dawson Street in Dublin. It was built in 1710 as a town house residence for local property developer Joshua Dawson. In April 1715 it was bought by the City Council for use as the official residence of Dublin's Lord Mayor. The nominal ground rent included "a loaf of double refined sugar at Christmas"! (The Irish Image Collection/Corbis/42-19019409)

FAR RIGHT: Enniscoe House is a typical Georgian house set beneath the towering Mount Nephin, at Castlehill, near Ballina, County Mayo, with spectacular scenery and grounds, including a Victorian walled garden, that extend to the banks of Lough Conn. It is now a luxury hotel and self-catering vacation center. (Michael St. Maur Sheil/Corbis/SH004544)

FAR LEFT: A typical scene in many of Ireland's country villages, towns, and harbors, where terraces of what would otherwise be drab houses are brightened with powerful contrasting color schemes. This is a road in Eyeries, a village on the Beara Peninsula in County Cork.
(Philippa Wood/fotoLibra/451848)

LEFT: A typical small farm cottage near the village of Dunquin on the Dingle Peninsula, County Kerry, enjoying views overlooking the Blasket Islands, near Garraun Point, Ireland's most westerly settlement.
(The Irish Image Collection/Corbis/42-19019551)

OVER PAGE: Waterfront Hall was completed in 1997 and has played a key role in Belfast's economic and social development since then. It is the centerpiece of the prestigious Lanyon Place development on the banks of the River Lagan and includes the 200-room Hilton International Hotel. The multipurpose venue plays host to musicals, concerts, operas, theater, conferences, and celebrations.
(Richard Cummins/Corbis/CU943570)

The Arts in Ireland

The Arts in Ireland

The arts of Ireland—performing and static—are as rich in their depth and diversity as the very culture of the island itself and its peoples. Ireland is world-famous for its poets and writers (Joyce, Wilde, Yeats, Shaw and so forth), but less so for its statuary and sculpture, its indigenous music and dance, its galleries, and the contribution of international rock music performers (such as U2) and movie stars (like Pierce Brosnan) to the world's entertainment scene.

Being static, or permanent, Irish monuments and statues are appreciated by local inhabitants and visitors alike, and many are specific-to-location. One of the best-known monuments is the statue of Daniel O'Connell, most celebrated of all Irish political leaders, which stands in the main thoroughfare of Dublin City that bears his name. While O'Connell could draw and inspire a mass political meeting, the numbers of people listening would have been dwarfed by the 100,000 crowds of rock music fans crammed into the grounds of Slane Castle in County Meath, a few miles upstream from the famous Battle of the Boyne.

Throughout Ireland there are scores of art galleries and centers with fabulous collections that may be viewed by the general public, while the streets and squares of the main cities are host to fine sculptural works by famous and yet-to-be-famous artists.

Irish theater has roots stretching back to Celtic language performances. Theatrical productions tended to serve the political purposes of the administration of the time, whereas more recently (over the past four hundred years) a more diverse range of entertainments have been staged for wider audiences. Of particular note in the history of Irish theater has been the establishment and influence of the Abbey Theatre (formed in 1899 as the Irish Literary Theatre), although over the last twenty years a new wave of theater companies has arrived to challenge the Abbey's dominance.

FAR LEFT: Faroukh Ruzimatov dancing in the Kirov Ballet production of *Swan Lake*, at the Royal Dublin Society (RDS), Simmonscourt, Dublin. The RDS was founded on June 25, 1731, "to promote and develop agriculture, arts, industry, and science in Ireland."
(Robbie Jack/Corbis/ RJ002227)

LEFT: There has been a theater on the present site of the Cork Opera House (shown here with its modern glass façade) since 1855. It stood for a hundred years until it was destroyed in a fire in 1955, and was rebuilt. Incorporating a 1,000-seat auditorium and an orchestra pit for seventy musicians, it offers audiences a world-class program across all disciplines in the performing arts.
(Rachel Royse/Corbis/AAJK001116)

RIGHT: Affectionately known as the "Matcham Masterpiece" after theatrical architect Frank Matcham, the Grand Opera House in Belfast has certainly seen some highs and lows since its curtain first rose on December 23, 1895. Since then it has offered audiences a wide program of entertainment, including opera, drama, pantomime, movies, and musicals.
(Geray Sweeney/Corbis/AABS001108)

FAR RIGHT: Over the years, the Grand Opera House, part of the interior of which is shown here, suffered austerity following two world wars, was at the center of victory celebrations, lost the commercial battle against emerging television technology, was targeted by the IRA's bombs, was forced to close in 1972, but became the first building in Belfast to be listed as being of historical and architectural importance. It reopened with government funding and control as part of a massive regeneration program that affected the whole of Belfast city center.
(Geray Sweeney/Corbis/AABS001212)

LEFT: Among the eclectic examples of statuary to be found in Ireland's towns and cities is this gaudy, colorful depiction in Dublin's Merrion Square of the great playwright, poet, and novelist Oscar Fingal O'Flaherty Wills Wilde (1854–1900).
(The Irish Image Collection/Corbis/42-19019259)

ABOVE: A statue of poet Anthony Raftery (1784–1835) in Craughwell, County Galway, where he died. Despite having lost his sight as a result of smallpox as a child, Raftery wandered the countryside, making a living by entertaining at the great mansions of the Anglo-Irish gentry. He was often referred to as "The Blind Poet."
(The Irish Image Collection/Corbis/42-19784471)

CAROLAN
1670-1738

FAR LEFT: The Gaiety Theatre, South King Street, Dublin, specializes in operatic and other musical productions, with occasional dramatic shows. The theater itself was opened in late 1871, extended by Frank Matcham in 1883, and has undergone more recent refits.
(Paul O'Kane/fotoLibra/441674)

LEFT: The statue of Irish political leader Daniel O'Connell (1775–1847) commands the south end of the Dublin street that bears his name. The statue was designed and sculpted for the most part by John Henry Foley, who died in 1874, and was completed by his assistant Thomas Brock. It was unveiled in 1882.
(Nigel B. Coates/fotoLibra/495882)

RIGHT: A statue of King William III in the grounds of Carrickfergus Castle, County Antrim, It was at Carrickfergus that the English king made his celebrated landing on June 14, 1690, and headed straight to Belfast where he defeated the forces of his father-in-law James II at the Battle of the Boyne. (Roger Bradley/iStockphoto/6094902)

FAR RIGHT: This statue of a robed figure, armed with sword and scales, the symbols of justice, stands above the main entrance archway at Dublin Castle, in the old part of Dublin. (Michael Nicholson/Corbis/MN001189)

FAR LEFT: A memorial to nineteenth century famine victims stands on the Custom House Quay in Dublin. The 1997 memorial, made up of six bronze figures, is by sculptor Rowan Gillespie. During the "famine" period of 1845 to 1852, and the associated starvation, mass emigration, and political repercussions, Ireland's population fell by between twenty and twenty-five percent.
(The Irish Image Collection/Corbis/42-19785387)

CENTER: The dramatic memorial to the courageous performance of the United Irishmen (rebels) against the British forces in the Battle of New Ross, June 5, 1798. At one stage, the rebels, armed mostly with nothing but pikes, broke up a British cavalry charge.
(K. Stuart/iStockphoto/2704900)

LEFT: Jeanne Rynhart's sculpture of the fictitious fishmonger "Molly Malone," from the famous Dublin anthem, was erected in Grafton Street to celebrate the city's millennium in 1988. Her ample cleavage soon had local wags offering nicknames, including "The Tart With the Cart" and "The Trollop With the Scallop." (There were many "millennium" celebrations held during the 1980s and 1990s, chosen somewhat arbitrarily by the Tourist Board to boost business during a depressed commercial period. The Dublin Millennium actually commemorated the submission of the King of Dublin to Mael Seachlainn II in 988, although this occurred in 989!)
(The Irish Image Collection/Corbis/42-19019217)

153

RIGHT: Depicting the Virgin Mary cradling the dead body of Christ, this sculpture of the Pietà, or the Thirteenth Station of the Cross, is situated on Sheep's Head headland in County Cork, looking over the Caha Mountains on the Beara Peninsula. (The Irish Image Collection/Corbis/42-19014188)

CENTER: This somewhat simplistic statue of St. Patrick, patron saint of Ireland, is a little off the usual tourist tracks, set in a crumbling dry stone wall enclosure near the Céide Fields on Downpatrick Head in County Mayo. (The Irish Image Collection/Corbis/42-19008872)

FAR RIGHT: Eamonn O'Doherty's intriguing 1995 sculpture entitled "To The Skellig" at Cahirciveen, County Kerry, shows four monks rowing a small boat to the tiny Skellig St. Michael monastery. (The Irish Image Collection/Corbis/42-19014254)

FAR LEFT: And now for something completely different… Within the scope of Ireland's burgeoning range of performing arts we see American symphonic rock band The Polyphonic Spree on the Main Stage at the Electric Picnic Boutique Music Festival in September 2007. The festival, one of many rock music shows held throughout Ireland, began as a one-day event in 2004 and is now a three-dayer held annually at the Stradbally Estate, County Laois.
(Kirsty Umback/Corbis/42-18866246)

LEFT: Almost every August since 1981, rock music concerts by world-renowned artists have taken place in the grounds of Slane Castle on the River Boyne, half a mile upstream from the tiny village of Slane, in County Meath. Here the crowd gathers for the Queen rock group's concert in 1986.
(Denis O'Regan/Corbis/RN001211)

OVER PAGE: At the RDS (Royal Dublin Society) ground on September 12, 2008, Leinster (in blue) dished out a massive beating to Edinburgh, 52 points to 6, in the Rugby Union Magners League.
(Nigel B. Coates/fotoLibra/495864)

Sports in Ireland

Irish sports are as diverse as any other aspect of life in Ireland today. Participation in sports may have declined of late, because of the increasing popularity of other pastimes such as playing computer games and watching TV, but nevertheless levels of spectating remain high, oddly enough because of the burgeoning increase in TV channels available and the 24/7 coverage devoted to some sports.

While Ireland contributes greatly to international games such as soccer, Rugby Union, golf, showjumping, and snooker, the biggest audiences are those for traditional Irish games, in particular Gaelic football (Ireland's most popular sport, measured in terms of match attendance) and hurling (second most popular). Gaelic football has been played for centuries, but was formally organized in the late nineteenth century. Now, the final of the senior championship can be expected to draw spectators numbering 80,000-plus, and its share of attendances across all sports events is more than a third, with its closest rival, hurling, claiming twenty-three percent.

Participation sports include several water sports, hockey, cycling, target shooting, and boxing, and one in particular merits a mention because of its unusual nature: the ancient sport of road bowling, in which participants throw, or bowl, a "cannonball" along a country lane over a specified distance, trying to use as few as possible throws along the way.

Sports attract betting, none more so than horse racing (in which Irish horses, trainers, and jockeys are perennially successful) and greyhound racing (which began in Ireland in 1927 and now boasts twenty licensed tracks).

RIGHT: Even Scotland's Edinburgh team that suffered such an overwhelming defeat by Ireland's Leinster would have to agree they need to go back to basics, which are (in much-simplified form) that Rugby Union is a game played with an oval ball by two teams of fifteen players. A match lasts for eighty minutes (plus stoppage time) with a ten-minute break at half-time. Points are awarded for scoring a "try" (when a player grounds the ball within his opponent's in-goal area) or by kicking the ball over the crossbar but between the posts of the opponent's goal. That's how simple it is, Edinburgh.
(Nigel B. Coates/fotoLibra/495864)

FAR RIGHT: Soccer (football) is played throughout Ireland. There are two national teams, the Republic of Ireland and Northern Ireland. Here, Republic of Ireland's Steve Finnan (in green shirt) avoids a tackle by Germany's Lukas Podolski during their Euro 2008 qualification match. Unfortunately, both Irish teams failed to qualify for the finals, while Germany were defeated 1-0 by Spain in the final.
(Bernd Weissbrod/epa/Corbis/42-19052524)

FAR LEFT: If you were playing soccer you would be shouting, "Hey, you can't do that!" But this is a Gaelic football match being played at Limerick, and the rules are different: in Gaelic football (with fifteen players each side) the ball is moved up the field by a combination of carrying, dropping then toe-kicking the ball into the hands, kicking, and hand-passing to team-mates. The object is to get the ball into the opponents' goal either above the crossbar in the H-frame, or (better) in the netted goal.
(Stephen Power/fotoLibra/495307)

LEFT: Gaelic football and hurling are the two most popular sports in Ireland. This is just a portion of the crowd of supporters crammed into the 82,300-capacity Croke Park, Dublin, stadium to watch the Gaelic football All Ireland Final, played every year in September.
(Sean Bonner/fotoLibra/495586)

LEFT: If you like your sports "ethnic" look no further than the All Ireland Road Bowling Championships. On this occasion the 1995 final was held on Cathedral Road, Armagh, Northern Ireland. Road bowling is an ancient Irish sport, in which players throw a 28-ounce bowl or "bullet" along a country road course up to two-and-a-half miles long, with the winner being the player who takes the fewest throws to complete the course. All the while the spectators offer helpful "advice." (Michael St. Maur Sheil/Corbis/SH001496)

FAR LEFT: It's a close-run race as the leading horses sprint for the finishing line at Gowran Park racecourse in County Kilkenny. Horseracing is perennially popular with Irish and visiting punters, who can enjoy the "sport of kings" at two courses in Northern Ireland and twenty-five in the Republic. (Noel Mealy/fotoLibra/495394)

LEFT: With the vast Atlantic Ocean as a backdrop, golfers prepare to putt out at Ballybunion Golf Club, County Kerry, considered to be one of the top ten links courses in the world. Tackling some of the very many courses in Ireland accounts for a high proportion of the visitors every year. (The Irish Image Collection/Corbis/42-19784587)

OVER PAGE: A St. Patrick's Day Parade in Dublin—epitomizing the Irish knack of combining a sense of culture and tradition alongside a great appetite for fun and spectacle. St. Patrick's Day is celebrated every year on March 17, except when it coincides with Holy Week, when (controversially) it has to be moved to another date. No panic, though: the next time this will occur is in 2160. (The Irish Image Collection/Corbis/42-19009194)

Living in Ireland

Living in Ireland

Life in the Republic of Ireland and Northern Ireland is full of contrasts, from the leisurely pace in countryside villages and towns to the fast-lane whirl of busy cities. The Irish certainly know how to enjoy themselves, and their fun-loving nature is just one of the features that attracts about nine million visitors to the island every year.

They love making music and listening to it in lively pubs, or in theaters, or in the jam-packed open-air rock concerts. A "quiet night in" doesn't seem part of their agenda—witness the somewhat raucous pubs in Dublin's Temple Bar district, and the warmth of the more traditional atmosphere in the bars of County Cork's Kinsale.

The Irish enjoy their food too, from the filling, traditional stews their forebears ate to the sophisticated cuisine offered by the increasing number of high-class restaurants. With the environment in mind they seek to reduce "food miles" and wastage by buying fresh ingredients locally, all of it to be washed down with creamy-topped stouts, such as Guinness, or fine wines provided by the world's vineyards.

As one would expect of an island so steeped in history and drama, there's so much to explore, to see, and to do for inhabitants and visitors alike. Throughout the year there are spectacular festivals and so-beloved parades, many of them themed to Irish history and heritage, for example, or to food and drink, or to arts and crafts, celebrating everything from literary pursuits to a love of oysters. But the main festival is St. Patrick's Day, March 17, celebrating one of the patron saints of Ireland. Surprisingly, the first St. Patrick's Festival was held only as recently as 1996 and grew from a one-day event to a five-day festival by 2006. One of the official aims of the festival is to "*provide the opportunity and motivation for people of Irish descent (and those who sometimes wish they were Irish) to attend and join in the imaginative and expressive celebrations.*" As the saying goes, "Everyone's Irish on March 17th!"

FAR LEFT: At night, it's fun all the way in Dublin's Temple Bar, the city's "cultural quarter" of narrow cobbled streets, a major tourist attraction. But the downside is the drunken, loutish behavior, mostly by tourists, that is encountered there, to the extent that in 1999 locals, attempting to maintain the bohemian atmosphere, pressurized the council to ban bachelor and bachelorette parties from the U.K. (David Bukach/fotoLibra/495356)

LEFT: The locals certainly know how to enjoy themselves with music and beer, to the benefit of tourists also. Here, musicians and friends gather at Cleary's Pub to relax and play Irish music, for which County Clare is well known. (Stephanie Maze/Corbis/AZ003910)

RIGHT: Blue mussel shells are indicative of a growing popularity of seafood dishes, particularly among visitors but also with locals. Of course, the seas around Ireland's coasts ensure good stocks of the main ingredients.
(Sanphire/iStockfoto/53548)

FAR RIGHT: Fresh vegetables (such as these on show at Dublin's Moore Street market) are a staple for the more traditional Irish dishes like stews and colcannon (similar to English bubble and squeak, with cabbage, leeks, mashed potato, onions, garlic, and chives—together with boiled ham or Irish bacon, if that is your fancy).
(Alex Ramsay/fotoLibra/441120)

GUINNESS

GACH LÁ

FAR LEFT: An inviting glass of Guinness in a Dublin pub. It's Ireland's best-selling alcoholic drink, popular with the Irish and tourists, but care and patience are required during pulling in order to serve a "perfect pint." The brewers advise that this should take 119.5 seconds with, traditionally, a period three-quarters of the way through the operation for the "black stuff" to stand before a "double-pour" creates a creamy head in a dome just over the top of the glass. Some bartenders will use the flow from the head of the tap to "draw" a shape (usually a shamrock) in the head, although purists frown upon this practice.
(George Philip/fotoLibra/443392)

LEFT: A traditional Irish pub in Clonakilty, County Cork. There would have been no mistaking what's on offer, whatever the language used on the poster!
(The Irish Image Collection/Corbis/42-19783088)

RIGHT: Irish dancing, broadly categorized as social dance ("set" dancing) or performance dance (traditionally referred to as stepdancing, as popularized by the world-famous show *Riverdance*), is enjoyed throughout Ireland, But it's serious business, too. Here, two light-footed girls participate in the All Ireland Dance Championships (2003). (Eva-Lotta Jansson/Corbis/DWF15-408875)

FAR RIGHT: Wrenboys celebrating the Traditional Christmas Festival in County Limerick. The festival takes place on St. Stephen's Day, December 26, and involves participants throughout Ireland dressing up in straw masks and colorful clothing, accompanied by traditional Irish music, as they parade through towns and villages. (Stephen Power/fotoLibra/495425)

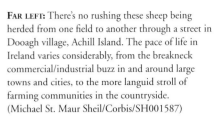

FAR LEFT: There's no rushing these sheep being herded from one field to another through a street in Dooagh village, Achill Island. The pace of life in Ireland varies considerably, from the breakneck commercial/industrial buzz in and around large towns and cities, to the more languid stroll of farming communities in the countryside. (Michael St. Maur Sheil/Corbis/SH001587)

LEFT: A tricky operation, as island farmers transport sheep to the mainland by dinghy. Understandably, the sheep are not anxious to go for a dip in choppy waters. (The Irish Image Collection/Corbis/42-19012636)

RIGHT: A tranquil cruise along one of Ireland's many canals, the Jamestown, which forms a link between the River Shannon and Lough Nanog to the south of Drumsna, County Leitrim.
(The Irish Image Collection/Corbis/42-19010482)

FAR RIGHT: Happy with the slower pace of life in County Galway, this Irish farmer rides a horse-drawn, two-wheel chaise, or cart (or sometimes "chair"), unconcerned about holding up the traffic, because there is none. There have been many different designs of chaise/cart, intended for carrying people or goods, and drawn by one or more horses or other animals.
(Bertrand Rieger/Hemis/Corbis/42-19834694)

FAR LEFT: It doesn't get more isolated than this… A couple of tourists on a typical cycle track, The High Road, Inishmore, Aran Islands, contemplating whether to continue on toward some form of civilization, or take the easier option and turn back. (Jonnie Morgan/iStockphoto/4476926)

LEFT: Apart from the unknown temperature, this could be Australia, or Goa. But it's actually Rosslare Strand, County Wexford, one of the very many quiet, sandy beaches to be found along Ireland's craggy coastline. It claims to be the sunniest spot in Ireland, enjoying 300 hours more sunshine a year than anywhere else in the country. (Doorly/iStockphoto/3619237)

RIGHT: Golf courses such as this, the Westport on the shores of Clew Bay, just outside Westport Town in County Mayo, are a major attraction for both locals and vacationers. Golfers tend to speak in hushed tones to avoid spoiling the tranquillity of this wonderful countryside.
(Tony Roberts/Corbis/ OT001516)

Index